Islam:
the Empowering
of Women

Aisha Bewley

Ta-Ha Publishers Ltd
Unit 4, The Windsor Centre
Windsor Grove, West Norwood
London SE27 9NT, United Kingdom

© 1430 / 2009 Aisha Bewley

First published in Muharram 1420 / April 1999
and reprinted in Ramadan 1430 September 2009 by

Ta-Ha Publishers Ltd.
Unit 4, The Windsor Centre
Windsor Grove, West Norwood
London SE27 9NT, United Kingdom

URL: http://www.taha.co.uk/
e-mail: sales@taha.co.uk

Typesetting by Bookwork, Norwich

British Library Cataloguing in Publication Data
A catalogue record for this book is available from the British Library.

ISBN: 978-1-897940-75-4

Printed by Mega Printing, Turkey.
URL: http://www.mega.com.tr
email: info@mega.com.tr

Contents

By the Same Author

Books

Subatomic World in the Qur'an (Diwan Press)
Signs on the Horizons: The Sun, the Moon, the Stars
    (Zahra Publications)
A Glossary of Islamic Terminology (Ta-Ha Publishers Ltd)
The Islamic Will (Dar al-Taqwa)
    [Co-author with Hajj Abdal-Haqq Bewley and Ahmad Thomson]

Translations into English

The Noble Qur'an – a New Rendering of its Meaning in English
    (Bookwork) with Hajj Abdal-Haqq Bewley
Al-Muwatta' of Imam Malik (Madinah Press)
Ash-Shifa' of Qadi 'Iyad (Madinah Press)
The Foundations of Islam – *Al-Qawa'id* of Qadi 'Iyad
    (Madinah Press)
Handbook on Islam, Iman, Ihsan of Shaykh 'Uthman dan Fodio
    (Madinah Press)
Defence against Disaster – *Al-'Awasim min al-Qawasim* of Qadi Abu
    Bakr ibn al-'Arabi with a modern commentary. (Madinah Press)
The Islamic Book of the Dead (Hadith on the Garden and the Fire)
    (Diwan Press)

The Women of Madina – Vol. 8 of the *Tabaqat* of Ibn Sa'd
    (Ta-Ha Publishers Ltd)
The Men of Madina, Vol. 1 – Vol. 7 of the *Tabaqat* of Ibn Sa'd
    (Ta-Ha Publishers Ltd)

The Diwans of the Darqawa (Diwan Press)
The Meaning of Man of Sidi 'Ali al-Jamal (Diwan Press)
The Darqawi Way (the Letters) of Mulay al-'Arabi ad-Darqawi
    (Diwan Press)
Self-Knowledge (Commentaries on Sufic Songs) (Diwan Press)
The Tawasin of Mansur al-Hallaj (Diwan Press)
The Seals of Wisdom – *Fusus al-Hikam* of Ibn al-'Arabi
    (Diwan Press)

Preface

For years people have been asking me to write or speak on 'the role of women in Islam'. I have always inwardly groaned at the prospect since it has always seemed perfectly obvious that the proper title should be 'the role of the human being in Islam' – how to become a whole, vibrant human being, worshipping our Creator by being in tune with the unfolding wonder of existence and establishing an arena in which social and political justice can be achieved by the implementation of Allah's Message. What is more important than a male/female dichotomy is the 'abd/rabb dichotomy: the slave and the Lord.

Nonetheless, the great amount of ignorance of and disinformation about Islam which is constantly being reinforced by the media has finally forced me to actually examine the issue. What do we discover when examining modern literature on the topic? In the West we find the Oppression of Women in Islam in its various guises – more often than not harping on cultural matters (which are not specific to Islam) and accusing Islam of being responsible for them. On the Muslim side – usually as a reflex reaction to the Oppression of Women in Islam – we find various ripostes to this, mostly written by men, about how Islam Came to Liberate Women (from their inferior position in a pagan environment without reference to the modern situation), True Fulfilment Lies in Being a Housewife, Women Aren't Physiologically Really Up to the Level of Men (which historically is not an Islamic, but a Judaeo-Christian view) and Women Should be Neither Seen Nor Heard (justified by the dubious assertion that men are so weak and testosterone-ridden that they are incapable of self-control).

Having been involved in studying and translating texts from the early period of Islam, these themes simply do not ring true.

1

The women then were not like this. The Companions were not like this. The Prophet, may Allah bless him and grant him peace, was not like this. They were vibrant, dynamic people who devoted themselves to the implementation of Islam.

Reading historical sources throughout the centuries of Islamic history, we find lots and lots of women active in all areas of life, and then suddenly it stops. What happened? How and why have things changed in the last three hundred years to the extent that it is unusual to find women involved in Islamic sciences and, unlike in the past, very few Muslim men would even consider being taught by a Muslim woman? This is a phenomenon which requires in-depth research. It seems that it stems from various factors, some of which originated from outside the Muslim community and some from within:

- a re-assertion of pre-Islamic patriarchy;

- the adoption and emulation of the pre-Islamic practices of conquered peoples (Byzantine, Persian and Hindu). For instance, the adoption of the Byzantium gynaeceum which became the Ottoman harem;

- the infiltration of Western ideas, including the view of women as inferior (which was the Western position on women until fairly recent times);

- an active policy on the part of the colonialists to keep women (and indeed the Muslims as a whole) down;

- a legacy of colonialism: that Islam is 'barbaric' while European, Western customs and traditions are 'civilised'. This is reinforced by the ruling elites who inherited the mantle of colonial power, (while being shackled by debt);

- ressentiment – first allowing oneself to be defined by this 'barbaric/ civilised' dichotomy and then defending it, thus giving it a reality which it did not have to begin with.

This certainly is a syndrome which requires study.

There is yet another problem we have to deal with. In most cases these days modern Muslim thought is, in fact, Western thought dressed up in Islamic clothes. This is because the Western form of education has become prevalent world-wide. So we need to make a radical shift in our approach, take ourselves off the normal auto-pilot mode of thought. We need to actually **look** at what we are doing.

Virtually anybody educated in the modern "western" education system has developed a way of structuralist thinking which has three basic characteristics:

- 1) We think in structures. We build up our picture of things by making them into rigid forms, methodologies, categories, etc.

- 2) The dynamic of our thinking is dialectical, that is: thesis – antithesis – synthesis. This provides the illusion of movement, but there is no more movement than the rat running around a treadmill. So we posit: Western thought – and we put up an antithesis of it – "Islamic thought", but this Islamic thought is merely a reaction to and mirror image of the western thought, and so we come up with: Modernist Islam.

- 3) Mythic objectivity – or perhaps, scientific method. It implies in human experience that you can look 'out there' and analyse the other or the object, and you can take it to pieces and examine it, quantify it and define it objectively. This, of course, is part of structuralism. But in fact modern physics has told us that the observer has an effect on what he observes, and is not separate from 'it'.

When any of us thinks, these characteristics come into play. So the modern world fixes things, codifies them, tries to make them objective and absolute. In fact, reality is more flexible. Islam is very flexible. There is not one narrow and fixed form into which everyone must fit. Islam is a template with a great

3

deal of scope in it. The Prophet said, "My Companions are like stars. Whomever of them you follow, you will be guided." And they all had very different personalities. The wives of the Prophet also had very different personalities – from Khadija the businesswoman, to A'isha, the scholar who was very fiery and ready to lead an army, to Umm Salama, who was a model of reasoned calm intelligence, to his daughter Fatima, who was very content with quietly looking after the home. They were all wonderful. They were all extraordinary. No one said: "You must be like me to be okay." No one said: "If you don't dress like me, you're in trouble."

The excessive focus on Women As An Issue has got to change – or rather we must revert to what the Prophet brought – because it sidelines the whole impetus of Islam into nothing more significant than sorting out household affairs. In the past among the Turkic peoples, it was very common for women to act as regents while their husbands were away (a natural extension of overseeing the household), which means that by empowering her, he in turn was empowered to go and change society. She, being empowered and educated, would pass this on to her children who in turn would be empowered and go out and change society. Thus we have energy, dynamism and vibrancy. The alternative is all too often embittered or neurotic women imprisoned in their homes, expending all their efforts in trying to control their families and taking out their frustrations on them – and then the men are enslaved to this mutually debilitating emotional bondage. The social project goes down the drain.

A symptom of this is the EXCESSIVE concentration on the Issue Of Women's Dress – particularly on the part of men. It seems that women's dress has been transformed into the badge of Islamic identity. You do not define your identity as a Muslim by a piece of cloth – which is not to say take it off altogether. There is no doubt that it is necessary for women to be modestly dressed as indicated by the Prophet. But this is not the sole zone of action for the Muslim – there are more important issues which should attract our energy. The Prophet, may Allah bless him and grant him, peace, discussed men's dress more than he did women's dress. The constant and almost exclusive focus on women's dress has become a distraction from the real issues about which the Muslims should be much more passionate – like usury, social justice, and the actual implementation of Islam in a real way.

The first fundamental right any woman or man has is to be a free human being, able to fulfil the role for which she or he was created: to worship the Creator in the manner shown us by His Messenger, may Allah bless him and grant him peace. This exists nowhere at the present moment. And what is more alarming is that this crucial issue tends to be ignored in favour of a fixation on the minutiae of Women's Dress and Domestic Role. People ignore the fact that neither the man nor the woman is empowered in modern society. This tragic state of affairs was foreseen a hundred and fifty years ago by Alexis de Tocqueville when he wrote *Democracy in America*:

> "The will of man is not shattered, but softened, bent and guided: men are seldom forced by it to act, but they are constantly restrained from acting: such a power does not destroy, but it prevents existence: it does not tyrannize, but it compresses, enervates, extinguishes, and stupefies a people, till each nation is reduced to be nothing better than a flock of timid and industrious animals, of which the government is the shepherd." (p. 580).

This scenario is one which confronts Muslims as well as non-Muslims, particularly because most Muslims have taken on the Western method of thought – especially liberal individualism, which goes some way to explaining the excessive concentration on domestic rather than social issues. Often today we find that 'Islamic' has been tacked on to a Western concept – so we find 'Islamic' democracy, capitalism, economics, etc.

Action of any sort in a social context presupposes a shared perception of the concepts involved in undertaking that action. We cannot act as human human beings until we know what we are doing and why we are doing it, even if only subconsciously.

Positions must be re-examined. The real, vivid, transformative tradition of Islam as a living blueprint for life, relevant in every age – which in the modern age is the only truly radical solution – has been virtually lost. The task facing the Muslims today is how to rediscover and implement this blueprint, a task which involves action in the arena of society as a whole. This will necessarily involve discarding certain misconceptions which have been foisted onto the Muslims from the West. As Ibn 'Ata'llah says:

Nothing leads you on like illusion.
You are free when you despair of it.
You are a slave when you are eager for it.

It is time to re-examine the sources and re-assess how Muslim women in the past acted so that we can escape the limiting perspectives which have come to be the norm. To this end, we will examine three perspectives: the Scholarly Woman, the Political Woman, and the Spiritual Woman.

Aisha Bewley
Summer 1419/1998

The Scholarly Woman

'A'isha, the wife of the Prophet, said, "How splendid are the women of the Ansar. Modesty did not prevent them from becoming learned in the *deen*."

There is no doubt that Islam stresses the importance of knowledge. Everyone is familiar with the famous saying of the Prophet, may Allah bless him and grant him peace, "Seek knowledge, even in China." The Qur'an also commands us to seek knowledge. Allah says: *"Say: 'Lord, increase me in knowledge.'"* (20:114)

The importance of knowledge and its consequences is expressed throughout the Qur'an: *"Only those with knowledge will understand it,"* (29:43) and *"And they say, 'If only we had listened or used our intellects we would not have been among the people of the Blaze."* (67:10)

The list of *ayats* about this goes on and on. Without knowledge you will not fear Allah and will not understand, and hence are likely to end up in the Fire. The people of knowledge are 'the heirs of the Prophets', as the Messenger of Allah said. He also said, "Wisdom adds honour to the noble and exalts the slave until he attains to the level of kings." He also said, "A single *faqih* is more formidable to Shaytan than a thousand worshippers." This is because the one with knowledge can distinguish between the *halal* and the *haram*, and see the perils and machinations of Shaytan and thus avoid the traps he sets.

This command to seek knowledge is one which is directed to women as well as men.

Of course, 'A'isha's knowledge of the *deen* is famous. The Prophet, may Allah bless him and grant him peace, told his

7

Companions: "Take half your *deen* from Humayra' ('A'isha)." And the accounts we have from the Companions attest to the incredible amount of knowledge she possessed.

Abu Musa al-Ash'ari said: "Whenever we, the Companions of the Prophet, encountered any difficulty in the matter of any *hadith* we referred it to 'A'isha and found that she had definite knowledge about it."

'Urwa Ibn az-Zubayr stated: "I did not see a greater scholar than 'A'isha in the learning of the Qur'an, shares of inheritance, lawful and unlawful matters, poetry and literature, Arab history and genealogy.

Ibn al-Jawzi mentioned in the *Cream of the Cream* from Hisham ibn 'Urwa that 'Urwa said to 'A'isha, "Umm! I am not surprised at your knowledge of poetry since you are the daughter of Abu Bakr and he was the most knowledgeable of people (in poetry), but I marvel at your knowledge of medicine." She struck him on the shoulder and said, "The Messenger of Allah, may Allah bless him and grant him peace, was ill at the end of his life while the delegations of Arabs were coming to him from every direction. They prescribed things for him and I would treat him. It came from that."

Al-Qasim ibn Muhammad said, "'A'isha undertook *fatwa* (giving legal opinion) in the khalifates of Abu Bakr, 'Umar, 'Uthman and so on until she died."

In the *Shade of the Cloud* by Abu 'Abdullah al-Ghafiqi about 'A'isha, "She had the most transmissions and the most *fiqh* of those who gave *fatwa*. She was sought out by people from the furthest lands for the knowledge of the *Sunna* and what is obligatory. She related all the poetry of the Arabs with purity. She was wonderful in *tafsir* (commentary on Qur'an) and eloquent expression. She had the most ample portion of knowledge of medicine." She transmitted to at least 77 men and 8 women, of whom 14 (11 men and 3 women) were related to her.

In *The Commentary of the Muhammadan Path* by an-Nabulisi, he writes, "There is no blame at all for a woman to

8

become involved with any aspect of seeking knowledge and teaching it ... 'A'isha used to interpret the sciences and provide information on obscure matters to outstanding men. She corrected a group of Companions in many *hadiths* – they include: 'Umar and his son, Abu Hurayra, Ibn 'Abbas, 'Uthman ibn 'Affan, 'Ali ibn Abi Talib, Ibn az-Zubayr, Zayd, Abu'd-Darda', Abu Sa'id, al-Bara', Fatima bint Qays and others."

'Urwa said, "I never saw anyone with more knowledge about the *halal* and the *haram*, general knowledge, poetry and medicine than 'A'isha." Masruq said, "I saw the Companions asking 'A'isha about shares of inheritance." (Al-Hakim)

This was not limited to 'A'isha. It was like that with the rest of the Prophet's wives and the female Companions – like Umm Sulaym, Umm ad-Darda', Fatima bint Qays al-'Adawiyya, and other women after them. People used to receive knowledge and instruction from these women as they received it from men. This is confirmed in the books of *hadith,* history and biographical collections (*Tabaqat*).

The Prophet was keen to see that women were educated in Islam as well as the men. Women can be educated by men and we have an illustration of this when the Prophet sent 'Umar ibn al-Khattab to inform the women of the Ansar of the basis of Islam. In Ibn Sa'd's *Kitab at-Tabaqat al-Kabir*, Umm 'Atiyya reports that when the Messenger of Allah came to Madina, he ordered the women of the Ansar to gather in one house, and sent 'Umar ibn al-Khattab to them to convey the teachings of Islam.

Al-Bukhari deals with the chapter of the Imam warning the women and teaching them. In it he mentioned that Ibn 'Abbas said that the Prophet went out with Bilal. "The Prophet thought that he had not been heard, so he gave some admonishment to the women." Ad-Dimamini stated, "This is the basis for the presence of women at meetings and assemblies with the precondition that they are safe from temptation."

We will briefly mention a few outstanding women in this field:

Asma' bint Abi Bakr, the sister of 'A'isha

According to the *Isaba,* 'Umar asked Asma' bint Abi Bakr about dream interpretation. She transmitted things on that as well as other topics. Al-Qastallani (1:295) says in his commentary on the chapter of washing blood in the *Sahih* in regard to Asma', "She knew the science of dream interpretation. Ibn Sirin learned it from Ibn al-Musayyab, and Ibn al-Musayyab took it from Asma' and Asma' learned it from her father." In this chain of transmission, we have Ibn al-Musayyab learning from Asma'.

Umm ad-Darda'

Al-Qastallani also mentioned that 'Awn ibn 'Abdullah said, "Umm ad-Darda' came to us and we reported *hadith* in her presence. We asked, 'Have we bored you, Umm ad-Darda'?' She said, 'You have not bored me. I sought worship in Madina, and I have not found anything more pleasing to me than mutual reminding of knowledge,' or she said, 'mutual reminding of *fiqh.'"*

Many women excelled in this knowledge right from the very beginning. Take the example of this woman: Ibn 'Abdu'l-Barr mentioned that 'Umar ibn al-Khattab ordered, "Do not make the dower of women more than forty *awqiya,* even if it is the daughter of someone with paternal relatives, i.e. Zayd ibn al-Husayn al-Harithi. If it is more, I will put the extra into the treasury." A rather tall woman with a somewhat broad nose who was in the line of women stood up and said to him, "It is not like that." He said, "Why?" She said, "Because Allah says, *'and if you have given her a large amount, do not take any of it'* (4:20)." 'Umar said, "The woman is right and the man is wrong."

If we move on to the next generation, we find more outstanding women:

'Amra bint 'Abdu'r-Rahman: She was close to 'A'isha. She was one of those who gave legal opinions in Madina in the generation after the Companions. She was the foremost expert on the traditions of 'A'isha. Her opinion overrode the views of other authorities. Ibn Sa'd refers to her as an *'alima* or scholar. In the *Muwatta'* she is taken as the primary authority for three legal issues: the prohibition against digging up graves, the ban on selling unripe fruit, and the effect of crop damage on the sale of agricultural produce. In one case, she reversed the decision of her nephew to cut off the hand of a man who stole some iron rings. Thus we see that her opinion and authority were accepted on matters such as business transactions and punishments (*hudud*). Malik takes her as a legal precedent for details on the *hajj*. Clearly, then, her legal knowledge extended to all areas of *fiqh*.

Umm Waraqa: She collected and recited the Qur'an and may have assisted 'Umar in assembling the text.

Hafsa bint Sirin: She was the sister of the famous *Tabi'*, Muhammad ibn Sirin. She memorised the Qur'an at the age of twelve and her expertise was such that her brother would ask her how to read difficult or obscure passages. She read one-half of the Qur'an each night. She prayed and fasted incessantly. She was considered more intelligent than her contemporaries, al-Hasan al-Basri and her brother Ibn Sirin. She died after 100/718 at the age of 70 or 90. She is referred to as a traditionist, legist, and Sufi.

Before moving on to a more detailed analysis of the transaction of the transmission of knowledge, we will mention a few more outstanding women scholars to illustrate the fact that the role of women in the transmission of knowledge continued through the centuries. Generally speaking, in the Muslim world of the early medieval times, there was not any bar or prohibition on women pursuing studies – on the contrary, Islam encouraged it. As a result of this, many women became famous as religious scholars, writers, poets, doctors and teachers in their own right.

Nafisa bint al-Hasan (d. 208/824): She was a descendant of 'Ali, and was such an authority on *hadith* that Imam ash-Shafi'i sat in her circle in al-Fustat when he was at the height of his fame in Egypt. In his will, he insisted that his bier stop at her house on the way to the graveyard.

Karima bint Ahmad al-Marwaziyya: She lived to be a hundred and died in Makka in the middle of the fifth/eleventh century. She was the foremost authority on the text of al-Bukhari because of the excellence of her sources.

Shuhda bint Abi Nasr Ahmad al-Ibari (d. 574/1178): She was considered to be one of the best scholars of her age. She was known as *al-Kâtiba* (the writer) and *Fakhr an-Nisa'* (Glory of Women). She taught al-Bukhari and other works to large numbers of students. She lectured publicly in one of the main mosques of Baghdad on various topics.

Zaynab bint ash-Sha'ri (d. 615/1218): She met and received *ijazas* from a number of scholars, and Ibn Khallikan received an *ijaza* from her.

'A'isha bint Muhammad ibn 'Abdu'l-Hadi: She had a position in the transmission of *hadith* unequalled by many men. Born in Damascus in the early 8th/14th century, at the age of 4 she was brought before Abu'l-'Abbas Ahmad ibn al-Hajjar, a prominent *muhaddith,* or *hadith* scholar. She learned two small collections from him. Then she studied Muslim's *Sahih* collection with 'Abdullah ibn Hasan and others, and the *Sira* of Ibn Hisham. She collected *ijazas*[1] from scholars in Aleppo, Hama, Nablus and Hebron, and she became someone whom the travelling scholars sought out. She was one of Ibn Hajar's teachers. The historian Ibn al-'Imad called her the "*muhadditha* of Damascus" and said that she was the most reliable in transmission of the people of her time.

Other women achieved distinction as transmitters of *hadith*, like Khadija bint Ibrahim ibn Ishaq ad-Dimashqiyya, who died in 803/1400-1401. When she died, she was the sole authority for al-Qasim ibn 'Asakir. There was Maryam bint Ahmad (d. 805/1402-3) and Fatima bint Khalil (d. 838/1434), both of whom had *mashyaka*s composed for them (lists of those on whose authority they transmitted *hadith*.) Fatima was one of Ibn Hajar's teachers. Thus we see that these women were active participants in the live transmission of knowledge.

Umm Hani Maryam (778-871/1376-1466): Her grandfather took her to listen to at least nine teachers in Makka and Cairo and she received *ijazas* from twelve others. She memorised the Qur'an and studied most of the six books of tradition, especially al-Bukhari, and an abridged work of *fiqh*. Each of her four sons specialised in one of the four schools of *fiqh*. Her second husband was appointed to administer her grandfather's *waqf* (trust). When he died she inherited the management of it. In this capacity, she purchased a large property. When other members of the family disputed the validity of the transaction as well as her competence, she was vindicated, thus demonstrating the competence of women to manage large *waqf* properties.

Adh-Dhahabi related from at least three women, and as-Safadi (d. 764/1362) had *ijazas* from at least eight women. Ibn Hajar had fifty-three women teachers and mentioned twelve

---

1. An *ijaza* is a certification, by a teacher that a particular student was qualified to teach a particular subject or to transmit a specific book or collection of traditions.

women who were *musnida* (transmitters of a collection of traditions). As-Subki (d. 771/1370) had nineteen women among his 172 teachers. As-Suyuti (d. 911/1505) had thirty-three women among the 130 of his sources for *hadith*.

Hadith was the main field of scholarly prominence for women, where accurate memorisation was the major criterion of success. *Fiqh*, however, centred around *munazara*, or disputation of points of law, which meant that fewer women took part in this field of knowledge. Nevertheless, women could also act as *muftis* and *faqihs*. In fourth/tenth century Baghdad we find two women who gave *fatwas*: **Umm 'Isa bint Ibrahim** (d. 328/939) and **Amat al-Wahid** (d. 377/987), daughter of the Shafi'i judge Abu 'Abdullah al-Husayn al-Muhamili.

Another woman learned in *fiqh* was **Fatima of Samarqand** who lived in Aleppo in the 6th/12th century. She corrected her husband's legal judgements.

In the 7th/13th century, two women were known for legal knowledge: **'Ayn ash-Shams bint Ahmad** of Isfahan (d. 610/1213) was a *faqiha,* and **Umm al-Baqa' Khadija bint al-Hasan** (d. 631/1243) was a *zahida* devoted to law.

In Ibn Hajar, only two women are noted for their *fiqh*: **Umm Zaynab Fatima bint al-'Abbas** (d. 714/1314) of Baghdad, a mystic poet and preacher who thoroughly understood Islamic law, and **Umm al-'Izz Nudar bint Ahmad** (702-730/1302-1329). Another female preacher was praised by Ibn Taymiyya for her knowledge of *fiqh* .

As-Sakhawi mentions several hundred women of learning. Knowledge of *fiqh* is cited in two cases: **'A'isha bint 'Ali** (761-840/1359-1436) (also known as **Umm 'Abdullah, Umm al-Fadl, and Sitt al-'Ayish**), a Hanbali scholar of Cairo. She had *ijazas* from a number of Syrian and Egyptian teachers, read Qur'an, and studied penmanship, history, tradition and poetry as well as law. Her students included Ibn Hajar al-'Asqalani and al-Maqrizi. The sources stress her understanding and intelligence.

There are three women in the 10th/16th century known for *fiqh*. One of them received an *ijaza* to act as a *faqih*. The Damascus sufi *shaykha*, 'A'isha al-Ba'uniyya bint Yusuf (d. 922/1516), the author of several books about *tasawwuf*, came to Cairo where she gave legal opinions and taught. There was also **Khadija bint Muhammad al-Bayluni** (d. 930/1523) in Aleppo, who followed the Hanafi school (although her father and brothers were Shafi'is). This clearly indicates that her knowledge was not family based.

As late as the 12th/18th century, we find **Zubayda bint As'ad** (d. 1194/1780), the daughter and sister of chief *faqihs* of the Ottoman Empire, who was also a poet in Persian and Turkish.

Not many women were involved in the field of *usul al-fiqh* (legal methodology) and *kalam* (theology). However, we do find at least one: **Zaynab at-Tukhiyya** (d. 894/1388), the daughter of 'Ali ibn Muhammad ad-Diruti al-Mahalli. She memorised the Qur'an when young, and was taught the books that were the core elements in the Shafi'i *madhhab* and grammar. When she married, she continued to study *hadith*: al-Bukhari and Muslim.

This scholarly activity was not restricted to the east, but was prevalent in the west as well, in Morocco and Mauritania, and further south. In a book by Dr 'Abdu'l-Hadi at-Tazi about the Qarawiyyin mosque in Fes, he says:

> "It was part of the foundation of one of the excellent ladies of Fes [Fatima bint Muhammad al-Fihri] who had precedence over other educated ladies. Moroccan history knows many names of the women who were famous for their scholarly activity – like al-Amira Tamima, the sister of 'Ali ibn Yusuf, who lived on the side of the Qarawiyyin; Khayrana al-Fasiyya who had a role in spreading the Ash'arite creed among the women of Fes; and the poetess Sara bint Ahmad ibn 'Uthman (750 AH). It was said that Ibn Salmun (741 AH) boasted of receiving her

ijaza. She exchanged poetry with Ibn Rashid al-Fihri. There was also the woman *faqih* and *mufti*, Umm al-Banin al-'Ubudiyya and her sister, the scholar Fatima, from the family whose men and women were equally famous, and the woman *mufti* Umm al-Banin. They attended the lessons of Shaykh al-'Abdusi (848 AH). Those ladies used to continue their studies in a special session they had. The Qarawiyyin had places which assisted the attendance of women to listen directly to the great shaykhs along with the students who listened to them.

The al-Andalus mosque in Fes was built by Maryam, the sister of Fatima. It later became a branch of the Qarawiyyin Mosque and became a centre of teaching. In the beginning of the fourth century after the *hijra* we find al-'Aliyya, the daughter of Shaykh at-Tayyib ibn Kiran teaching a circle there from behind a screen. She taught various subjects. Women attended her lessons after the *'Asr* prayer, and men before the *Dhuhr* prayer.

Women scholars and Sufis in southern Morocco and Mauritania included Fatima bint Muhammad al-Hilaliyya, Khadija bint Imam Muhammad al-'Atiq ash-Shanqiti, and Rabi'a bint Shaykh Muhammad al-Hadrami, the granddaughter of Shaykh Ma' al-'Aynayn ash-Shanqiti (b. 706/1307).

In Nigeria, Maryam, the daughter of Shaykh 'Uthman dan Fodio, composed many poems in Fulfulde in addition to a commentary on the legal compendium, the *Mukhtasar* of Shaykh Khalil, in Fulfulde. Also famous for her scholarship was his daughter Asma' who developed a method of instruction which we will mention shortly.

Of course, we also find women involved in more secular areas of knowledge. Ibn an-Nadim mentions some women grammarians. The 'Abbasid poet, Abu Nuwas, could recite the collected poems of fifty women poets. There is a book on medicine by an Indian woman, Rusa, and one on alchemy by an Egyptian woman. 'Ijliyya bint al-'Ijli was employed at the court of Sayf ad-Dawla (333-357/944-967) making astrolabes. In the field of calligraphy, Thana', a slave owned by the tutor of one of the sons of the Abbasid caliph, al-Mansur, was one of the two people he sent to be trained by the leading calligraphist of the day, Ishaq ibn Hammad. There are most probably many others in various fields of expertise. However, what we are primarily dealing with here is knowledge of the *deen*.

It is obligatory on a woman to acquire a full knowledge of her religious obligations such as prayer, fasting, *zakat, hajj*, as well as things like trade and transactions. If the husband is not able to supply this knowledge, she is under an Islamic obligation to go out in search of it. Shaykh 'Uthman dan Fodio, the famous Nigerian shaykh, says in *Irshad al-Ikhwan*, "If he refuses her permission, she should go out without his permission, and no blame is attached to her nor does she incur any sin thereby. The ruler should compel the husband to have his wife educated, just as he should compel him to give her adequate maintenance; indeed, knowledge is superior (to maintenance)."

In *Nur al-Albab*, he stated that the scholars who opposed women's education were hypocrites and "devils among men". He asks: "How could they leave their wives, daughters, and servants in the darkness of ignorance and error while they teach their students night and day! This is nothing but the pursuit of their selfish ends, because they teach their students only for show and out of pride. This is a great error." He added that teaching students is voluntary, unless there is no one else to do it, while teaching one's family is obligatory.

He said in the same book, "O Muslim women! Do not listen to those who are themselves misguided and who misguide others; who seek to deceive you by asking you to obey your husbands without asking you (first) to obey Allah and His Messenger. They say that a woman's felicity lies in her obedience to her husband; they say so only to fulfil their selfish ends and to fulfil their wishes through you. They compel you to do things which neither Allah nor His Messenger has originally imposed on you, like cooking, washing clothes, and similar things, which are among their numerous wishes while they do not in the least demand of you to perform the real duties imposed on you by Allah and His Messenger."

In *al-Irshad*, Shaykh Dan Fodio also says that women should demand their rights to education. Women, like men, have been created for the sole purpose of serving Allah, which cannot be obtained without true education: "Had the woman demanded her rights from her husband in the affairs of her religion and taken her case to the ruler, and demanded that either he educates her in the affairs of her religion or extends his permission to her to go out to learn, it would have been obligatory (by law) on the ruler to compel the husband to do so as he would compel him to give his wife her worldly rights, since religious rights are superior and preferred."

He also posed a question in *al-Irshad:* according to the Law, women have to go out in search of knowledge which husbands cannot provide; should the scholar who cannot secure separate seating arrangements go out into public to teach Islam, knowing full well that women are bound to attend his lectures? He says, "He should go out, but he should prevent intermixing of the men and women; and if such happens in his presence, he should put men on one side and women on the other side."

So Muslim women have the right to have education from their husbands and if not, to go elsewhere to get it. This is recognised by all reputable scholars. An early Muslim scholar of the Maliki school of law named Ibn al-Hajj, a severe critic of the over-liberal behaviour of the women in Cairo in his time, wrote: "If a woman demands her right to religious education from her husband and brings the issue before a judge, she is justified in demanding this right because it is her right that either her husband should teach her or allow her to go elsewhere to acquire education. The judge must compel the husband to fulfil her demand in the same way that he would in the matter of her worldly rights, since her rights in matters of religion are most essential and important."

✻✼✻✼✻

This brings us to a brief discussion of the educational system in Islam. The traditional educational system in Islam was informal: transmission of knowledge was dependent on a personal relationship with a teacher, not infrequently based on payment. Scholars received an *'ijaza*, a certification, by a teacher that a particular student was qualified to teach a particular subject or to transmit a specific book or collection of traditions.

The rise of the *madrasa* resulted in a certain formalisation of the process, but also opened up avenues for more people to study. Before the 5th/11th century, mosques were the principal venue for teaching circles. Teachers were paid by the students or by the largesse of the ruler or a benefactor. When the Nizamiyya *madrasa* was established in Baghdad in 459/1067, it provided stipends for teachers, and stipends and often living quarters for students. It opened up more possibilities for people to study by alleviating the financial burden of study.

In the Mamluk period, many women were associated with *madrasas* as their benefactors. In Mamluk Cairo, there were a minimum of five *madrasas* established by women. There were seven more established by women in Damascus. Sometimes the woman had the supervisory role in the administration of these institutions. Stipulations ensuring women's management of the *madrasa* were commonplace.

Not only were women endowing educational institutions, they were also taking an active part in learning. We hear from Ibn al-Hajj about the popular practice of women coming together with men in mosques to hear books read out by a shaykh. He said: "Consider what some women do when people [that is, men] gather with a shaykh to listen to books. At that point women come too, to hear the readings; the men sit in one place, the women facing them. It even happens at such times that some of the women are carried away by the situation; one will stand up, and sit down, and shout in a loud voice."

So well-known was the active participation of women in this area that as-Sakhawi commented of one woman, "I do not doubt that she had obtained *ijazas*, as her family was well-known for learning." He assumed that the women of his time were educated. Of the 1075 women listed in as-Sakhawi (*ad-Daw' al-Lami'*), a biographical dictionary of the 9th/15th century, 411 are listed with educational attainments: memorisation of the Qur'an, study with a particular scholar, or having an *ijaza*. Many entries are too brief for details. In as-Sakhawi we also find men receiving *ijazas* from learned women. Indeed, as-Sakhawi himself mentions having studied or received *ijazas* from 68 women.

A separate structure for teaching women was not necessarily required. In Mamluk Cairo, historians refer to girls whose fathers or brothers brought them to classes at a *madrasa*, and this was the most common route of access to learning for women: receiving instruction from male relatives who were scholars.

Sometimes houses were devoted to just women's instruction. There was a learned woman of the fifteenth century whose family seems to have committed itself especially to the religious education of women: "Her house was a gathering place for divorced and widowed women, and devoted to the instruction of young girls."

There was an institution called the Ribat al-Baghdadiyya, established in 684/1286 by a daughter of the Mamluk sultan Baibars. There were several others. They were places of residence for elderly, divorced or widowed women who had no where to live until their death or re-marriage. These places also provided education. The *shaykha* who administered such an institution routinely preached and taught *fiqh* to the residents.

This was what happened in the sophisticated, urban environment of Cairo. There are other possible methods of teaching more suited to rural and village situations. One is that developed by the daughter of 'Uthman dan Fodio, Asma'. She developed a method of bringing the women to her which has continued to exist until the present. She chose mature women of learning, intelligence, and reliable character, to head women's village units, and gave each leader a symbol of authority. They would go in groups, unescorted, to the capital, Sokoto, where Asma' received them and sorted out their problems. They were taught poems containing teaching which they memorised and then went home to teach. Poems were a common method of memorising and transmitting knowledge because they were easy to remember. Asma' was followed by Maryam, her half-sister. The khalif would consult her for advice on the affairs of Kano. Her influence lasted until the arrival of the British.

Jean Boyd describes the Modibo of Kware (Hajara) in 1404/1984, the great-great-granddaughter of Shaykh 'Uthman, born circa 1318/1901. She was married at the age of about twelve to the son of the ruler of Kasarawa, and continued her education under the direction of her teachers (one man and one woman). She was fluent in Arabic and Hausa and had a collection of books and manuscripts. She appointed women leaders and turbaned them. Each hamlet in Kware had pupils. They came to visit her from vast distances. Boyd saw a group of nine arrive in March 1984, bringing *sadaqa* (charity) in the form of grain. She would give advice and sort out rifts and misunderstandings. Women would come at night to hear her recite Qur'an. In the day she taught children (both boys and girls).

*****

Now the question is: what happened? At the end of the Mamluk period, there were large numbers of educated women with *ijazas* for teaching. But by the ninth century, it is hard to find a single one.

Something happened during this period. I personally think that European influence played a part in this, or perhaps a process of cultural infiltration (as there certainly has been from Hinduism in the Sub-continent) but it remains an area for investigation and study as was mentioned in the preface. It would be interesting to study the difference in the Sub-continent before and after 1857, when Mogul rule came to an end. It is probable that insecurity as a reaction to being colonised also played a part, as did ressentiment about the disparaging attitude of the colonialists. Certainly the change was less true of areas like Mauritania and northern Nigeria where direct European influence was not as strong, and where even today you still might well encounter women who know the entire *Muwatta'* of Imam Malik by heart.

As we have seen, there is no basis at all for barring women from education in the *deen*. Specifically, full knowledge about the obligations of the *deen* is an actual obligation for women as well as men. Of course, it is an obligation which many men fail to fulfil as well!

There are many pragmatic reasons for this being an obligation for women – beyond the obvious necessity of fulfilling one's personal religious duties. Women provide the first arena of instruction for children. The proverb, "The mother is the *madrasa*", focuses on this unavoidable fact. There is also the English proverb, "The hand that rocks the cradle rules the world." If the mother does not know the fundamentals of the *deen*, she simply is not going to pass them on to her children; and a few hours a week in a mosque school – which is often a VERY negative experience for the children involved – is not going to make up for that deficiency. The knowledge which the mother passes on is going to form the individuals who will form the society and eventually make up the political, social, and economic structure. Ultimately she is responsible for the cells which comprise the organism of society. Will they be imbued with knowledge or ignorance of the *deen*?

It is in this context that the saying of the Prophet, may Allah bless him and grant him peace, "Paradise lies at the feet of the mother," can best be understood – although this *hadith* is also taken to refer directly to the new-born child, newly arrived from the Garden, who will, if not brought up as a Muslim, subsequently become either a Jew, or a Christian, or a Fire-worshipper.

This obligation to pass on knowledge of the *deen* is particularly important now. The Prophet, may Allah bless him and grant him peace, said, "Among the signs of the Final Hour are the disappearance of knowledge and the establishment of ignorance..." (Bukhari). This is clearly happening now. The daily environment and social pressures – even in 'Muslim' countries, are more and more oriented towards non-Muslim values. If children do not receive instruction and an example from their home, they are going to have to start from scratch – and more often than not, they simply will not have the time.

It is crucial that women be given an arena for learning as well as men. It is the transmission of this knowledge that is important. And you have to want it – and if you want, you have to be determined to get it because modern society attempts to sideline it. And once you have it, you must transmit it.

As we have seen, up until the last 300 years, women took an active part in the transmission of knowledge – sometimes studying with and teaching men. It is an arena which somehow has been lost and needs to be reclaimed.

On a final note, in reference to the position of knowledge, Abu'd-Darda' reported that the Messenger of Allah said:

"Allah will make the path to the Garden easy for anyone who travels a path in search of knowledge. Angels spread their wings for the seeker of knowledge out of pleasure at what he is doing. Everyone in the heavens and everyone in the earth ask forgiveness for someone with knowledge, even the fish in the water. The superiority of a man of knowledge to a man of worship is like the superiority of the moon over all the planets. The people of knowledge are the heirs of the Prophets. The Prophets bequeath neither dinar nor dirham: they bequeath knowledge. Whoever takes it has taken an ample portion." (Abu Dawud and at-Tirmidhi)

This applies as equally to women as it does to men.

And when it comes to action, it is clear that incomplete knowledge is not a safe basis for effective action. Beneficial action, as we shall see in the next chapter, only stems from sound knowledge.

The Political Woman

Our first model of the political woman can be found in the
Qur'an: Bilqis, the Queen of Sheba. The Qur'an speaks
favourably of the Queen of Sheba and the manner in which she
consulted her advisors, who deferred to her better judgement on
how to deal with the threat of invasion by the armies of the
Prophet Sulayman. (Qur'an 27:32-35):

> She said, "O Council! Give me your opinion about
> this matter. It is not my habit to make a final choice
> until I have heard what you have to say." They said,
> "We possess strength and we possess great force. But
> the matter is in your hands so consider your com-
> mand." She said, "Kings, when they enter a city, lay
> waste to it and make its mightiest inhabitants the most
> abased. That is what they too will do. I will send them a
> gift and then wait and see what the messengers bring
> back."

She clearly possesses better judgement and discernment than
they have. First, she decides to test Sulayman by a gift to ascer-
tain whether he is a worldly king or a Prophet. This, in itself, is
a very fine illustration of her discernment and wisdom in such
matters.

Later, when she visits Sulayman and is confronted by her
throne, which had been transported and disguised, she says
about it, "It is very similar." She does not leap to rash judgements and deny or affirm it. She is measured in her assessment
and careful in her judgements. When the truth becomes clear to
her, she acts promptly and decisively, as befits a ruler. She
acknowledges the truth completely: *"O Lord, I have wronged*

25

myself but I have submitted with Sulayman to the Lord of all the worlds." (27:44) Commentators say that Sulayman confirmed her over her kingdom, and so we have no Qur'anic objection to a woman ruler.

Next we move to instances in the life of the Prophet and the Companions in our investigation of the political role of women. Our first instance here is the participation of women in the Pledge of 'Aqaba, where the people of Madina agreed to grant protection and support to the Prophet. This was the conclusion of a crucial treaty which had far-reaching consequences for Madina – militarily, economically and socially. And we find two women there taking part. According to Ibn Sa'd in his *Tabaqat*:

> Umm 'Umara Nusayba said, "The men clasped the hand of the Messenger of Allah, may Allah bless him and grant him peace, on the night when the Pledge of 'Aqaba was taken. Al-'Abbas ibn 'Abdu'l-Muttalib took the hand of the Messenger of Allah. Then I and Umm Mani' remained. My husband, 'Arafa ibn 'Amr called out, 'Messenger of Allah, these two women are with us to give allegiance to you.' The Messenger of Allah said, 'I take allegiance from them on the same basis which I took it from you, but I do not shake hands with women.'"

Another inevitable area of participation was war and military activity. In pre-Islamic times, women participated in tribal warfare, and women continued to fight alongside the Prophet Muhammad, may Allah bless him and grant him peace. Dozens of instances of this can be found, some involving auxiliary roles and some actually involving fighting. Some women, like Layla al-Ghifariyya, took part in battles by carrying water and nursing the wounded. Others, like Safiyya bint 'Abdul-Muttalib and Nusayba, fought and killed their enemies to protect themselves and the Prophet; and some, like Umm Dahhak bint Mas'ud at Khaybar, were rewarded with booty after the fighting was over in the same way as the men.

Al-Bukhari and Ahmad ibn Hanbal reported that ar-Rubayyi' bint Mu'awwidh said: "We used to participate in the battles with the Prophet of Allah. We gave water to the fighters, served them, and returned the dead and wounded to Madina."

Muslim, Ibn Majah and Ahmad ibn Hanbal reported that Umm 'Atiyya al-Ansariyya said: "I accompanied the Messenger of Allah seven times, guarding the camp, making the food, treating the wounded and caring for the sick."

In *al-'Utibiyya*, Malik said, "The women used to go out with the Messenger of Allah on raids with the reliable army in order to serve the fighters."

Az-Zuhri said, "The women used to be present with the Prophet in battles and give water to the fighters and treat the wounded."

Ibn Mardawiyya reported in his *tafsir* that Mu'adha al-Ghifariyya said, "I was close to the Messenger of Allah, may Allah bless him and grant him peace. I went out with him on journeys and I tended the sick and treated the wounded."

The *Tabaqat* of Ibn Sa'd has the biography of Umm Sinan al-Aslamiyya. She said:

> "When the Prophet wanted to go out to Khaybar, I came to him and said, 'Messenger of Allah, let me go out with you to bring the water and treat the sick and wounded if there are any wounded. I will look after the saddlebags.' The Messenger of Allah said, 'Go out in the blessing of Allah. You have some women companions who have spoken to me, and I have given them permission, both among your people and others. If you like, then go out with your people, or if you like, go with us.' I said, 'With you.' He said, 'Then be with Umm Salama, my wife.' She said, 'I was with her.'"

Ku'ayba bint Da'ud al-Aslamiyya treated the sick and
wounded. When Sa'd ibn Mu'adh was wounded on the Day of
the Ditch, he was taken to her to be cared for, and she treated
his wound until he died. She was at Khaybar with the Prophet
and he allotted her a man's portion.

Umm Ayman was present at Uhud. She gave water and treated the wounded. She was also present at Khaybar.

Al-Bukhari, in the Book on Expeditions, has the chapter of
the *jihad* of women, the chapter of the participation of women
in sea battles, the chapter of the man taking one wife to war
rather than another wife, the chapter on women going on exe-
peditions and their fighting alongside the men, the chapter of
women carrying waterskins to people in the expedition, the
chapter of women treating the wounded in the expedition, and
the chapter of the people bringing back the dead and wounded.
In it, he relates from Anas that when the people were routed
from the Prophet on the day of Uhud, "I saw 'A'isha and Umm
Sulaym with their dresses rolled up. I saw their anklets. They
were carrying waterskins on their backs. Then they returned
and filled them up. Then they came and emptied them into the
mouths of people."

Moving on to a more combative role, on the Day of Uhud,
the women were in the fortress of Hassan ibn Thabit when a
Jew came up to the fortress to spy. Safiyya bint 'Abdu'l-
Muttalib, the aunt of the Prophet and sister of Hamza, told
Hassan to go down and kill him. He was somewhat tentative
and so she took a pole and went down, carefully opened the
door, and killed the spy with the pole. (*Tabaqat*, Ibn Sa'd).
Later she went out with a spear which she shook in the faces of
the people.

Muslim reports from Anas that Umm Sulaym had a dagger
strapped to her waist at the Battle of Hunayn and stated, "I have
taken it so that if any of the idolaters comes near me, I will split
open his belly with it."

There was also Nusayba al-Ansariyya about whom 'Umar said, "I heard the Messenger of Allah say, 'I did not turn right or left in the Battle of Uhud but that I saw her fighting near me.'"

Nusayba was present at the Pledge of 'Aqaba, Uhud, al-Hudaybiyya, Khaybar, the Fulfilled *'Umra,* Hunayn and the Battle of Yamama in which her hand was cut off. She used both sword and bow. At Uhud, she received twelve or thirteen wounds, and a similar number at Yamama. In the course of her defence of the Prophet at Uhud, when only a handful of people remained to defend him, he noticed that she did not have a shield and saw a man retreating who had a shield. He told the man who was retreating, "Give your shield to the one who is fighting," pointing to her. The Prophet pointed out a man who had wounded her son, and she went and struck him on the leg and he went down. She said that the Messenger of Allah was smiling so that she could see his teeth. When she was badly wounded on the neck, he called to her son, "Your mother! Bind her wound! May Allah bless you, people of your house. The stand of your mother is better than the stand of so-and-so," and she asked him to ask Allah to make them his companions in the Garden, which he did.

She described the fight: "The horsemen did to us as horsemen do. If they had been on foot as we were, we would have trounced them, Allah willing. A man would come on his horse and strike at me and I would wield the shield against him and his sword. Then I would strike the hocks of his horse and he would fall off its back." When the Prophet returned to Madina he did not go home until he had news of her.

When Abu Bakr was khalif and the Muslims were setting out to fight the false prophet Musaylima in Yamama, she went to ask Abu Bakr for permission to join the expedition. He said, "We know your worth in war, so go out in the name of Allah." After the battle, Khalid ibn al-Walid treated the wound where her hand had been severed with hot oil.

In the Battle of Siffin, Hind, the wife of Abu Sufyan and mother of Mu'awiya, led the women in repulsing the attacking Byzantines when the Muslims broke ranks. There are many other instances as well.

In view of this history of women involved in the actual fighting, the participation of 'A'isha, the wife of the Prophet, in the Battle of the Camel was not particularly unusual. It is only at this point that a woman's presence in such events provokes criticism. However, the accounts date 150 years after the event, so there is bound to be a certain amount of colouring from later attitudes and partisan views, with everyone trying to justify his own position in this unfortunate event. But looking carefully at the accounts and remarks about the actual scene of the battle, there obviously was no particular objection to her presence as such at the time. Indeed, 'Ali is reported to have said afterwards, "If a woman could be khalif, 'A'isha would have been khalif." (*Identification of the Men* by Ibn 'Abdu's-Salam.)

Even after the Battle of the Camel, women are found fighting for both 'Ali and Mu'awiya at the Battle of Siffin some years later. (*'Iqd al-Farid*).

There was an incident during the conquests in Iraq when al-Mughira ibn Shu'ba was attacking the people of Maysan while the women were at the base camp. One of the women, 'Azda bint al-Harith, was worried that the enemy forces might prove too strong for the Muslim army. Therefore she came up with a plan to make the enemy think that reinforcements had arrived. All the women made banners out of their scarves and, under her leadership, marched chanting poems for the victory of Islam. When they reached the battlefield, the enemy thought that they were reinforcements and retreated.

There is no Qur'anic verdict on women's place on the battlefield, whether military or supportive, but clearly neither the Prophet nor the Companions objected to their presence and on occasion actually gave permission for them to join, which would amount to a consensus on its permissibility.

We also have women being put in charge of various important functions. We find a couple of instances of women acting as *muhtasibs* (market inspectors) in markets: According to *al-Isti'ab*, Samra' bint Nuhayk al-Asadiyya came to the Prophet and would go to the markets commanding good and forbidding evil. She would forbid the people to act incorrectly, using a whip which she had with her.

There was ash-Shifa bint 'Abdullah who was skilled in medicine, involved in public administration, and who had a strong presence in early Muslim history. Her real name was Layla. Ash-Shifa is a title derived from her profession as a healer: it means "healing." She embraced Islam before the *Hijra*, and was one of the earliest to migrate from Makka to Madina. She practised various forms of medicine and taught Hafsa, the wife of the Prophet, and others how to write. The Messenger of Allah used to visit her and gave her title to a house in Madina. His esteem for her company influenced the khalifs. 'Umar used to defer to her opinion. 'Umar's respect for her competence, character, and judgement led him to appoint her as an officer, or *wali*, in the administration of the marketplace. This makes her possibly the first Muslim woman to hold an official position in public administration, and certainly provides a precedent.

Before we move on to later historical periods, there is the vexed question of the oft-quoted *hadith* found in Ibn Hanbal: "A people who entrust power to a woman do not prosper." It is an isolated *hadith*, not found in the *Sahih* collections and was spoken about the ruler of the Sasanids (Boranduxt, d. 630-631 CE). It is not one which lays down a judgement (*hukm*) in *Shari'a*. Some believe it to have been forged after the Battle of the Camel to denigrate 'A'isha's role. We certainly do not find it used to censure women in positions of power early on. *Allahu a'lam.*

Moving on to another area, that of women acting as judges, al-Tabari said that women can be appointed to a judicial position to adjudicate in all matters. However Abu Hanifa excluded them from such weighty decisions as those involving the *hadd* and *qisas* (retaliation) punishments, and still other jurists said that women could not act as judges at all. Abu Hanifa is also reported to have said that they could only act in cases where their testimony would be acceptable. In al-Marghinani (a book on Hanafi *fiqh* of the sixth century AH), it states that a woman can be a judge in all trials except those dealing with *hudud* punishments. I have been told that the Maliki jurist, Ibn Rushd, took the same position as Abu Hanifa.

Under the Abbasids, Shaghab, the mother of al-Muqtadir bil-lah, who was acting as regent for her son, set up a legal court and put a woman judge in charge. The first day no one came. Then the woman appointed to the position brought the famous Qadi, Abu'l-Hasan, who stated that it was perfectly correct and in order, and then people came to the court.

There have certainly been women in positions of importance and leadership throughout Islamic history, and there have been many instances of women rulers who usually came to power after the death of their husbands or who acted as regents in their absence, especially among the dynasties which originated from Central Asia - the Seljuqs, the Mongols, the Mamluks, and the early Ottomans, etc. Some examples will serve to illustrate this. The most famous, of course, is Shajar ad-Durr.

Shajar ad-Durr: the Sultana, who was a sovereign ruler. She is sometimes thought of as the founder of the power of the Egyptian Mamluks. She married the Ayyubid Malik as-Salih and after the death of her husband, at first acting with Fakhr ad-Din Yusuf, she established control over Egypt. She led the resistance against the Seventh Crusade led by St. Louis, organised the defences, and captured him. For his release, Louis handed over Damietta and a ransom of 400,000 dinars. When the heir al-Mu'azzam died, the Mamluks met and agreed to appoint her sovereign. All edicts were issued in her name, but command of the army was given to Aybak. The oath of allegiance was given to her on 10 Safar 648/14 May 1250. The *khutba* was given in her name, and coins minted in the name of "The Queen of the Muslims". She later married Aybak and abdicated.

Shaghab: mother of al-Muqtadir, whom we mentioned above, ruled the Abbasid empire for a time. She held public audiences at which petitions and criminal matters were adjudicated. Governors and judges reported to her and she issued edicts.

Radiya: She ruled in Delhi a few years before Shajar ad-Durr ruled in Egypt. She succeeded her father, Sultan Shams ad-Din Iltutmish in 634/1236. She exercised full authority and led her troops in battle until she was supplanted by one of her brothers. Firishta, a sixteenth century historian of India says:

> "The Princess was adorned with every qualification required in the ablest kings, and the strictest scrutineers of her actions could find in her no fault but that she was a woman. In the time of her father, she entered deeply into the affairs of government, which he encouraged, finding she had a remarkable talent in politics. He once appointed her regent in his absence. When the emirs asked him why he appointed his daughter to such an office in preference to so many of his sons, he replied that he saw his sons giving themselves up to wine, women, gaming and flattery; that therefore he thought the government too weighty for their shoulders to bear; and that Radiya, though a woman, had a man's head and heart and was better than twenty such sons."

In 884/1479, Ibn 'Iyas, the chronicler of the later Mamluk period in Egypt provided this obituary for **Khawand (princess) Zaynab**, the sole wife of Sultan Inal (ruled 857-65/1453-61):

> "She was among the most noble princesses in rank. She enjoyed such prestige during the reign of her husband that she administered state affairs, influencing

both appointments and dismissals. She commanded wide respect, and possessed a substantial fortune ... the princess retained her honour and maintained her status until her death, at more than eighty years of age. Truly, she was among the notables of her time." [p. 122, Carl F. Petry, "Class Solidarity verses Gender Gain".]

Ghaziyya (d. 655/1257): She was one of the daughters of the Ayyubid sultan, al-Kamil, and was married to the prince of Hama. After her husband's death, she ruled in the name of her son. She is described by adh-Dhahabi as pious and modest.

Baghdad Khatbun bint an-Nuwan Chuban (d. 736/1335): She ruled over the Mamluks, was a female minister, rode in processions girded with a sword and rendered judgements. Her niece, **Dilshadh** (d. 752/1351) was the favourite wife of the ruler of Baghdad and was said to rule over Iraq.

Tandu bint Husayn (d. 822/1419): She became ruler of Baghdad after her husband was killed in 814/1411 (possibly at her instigation). Her rule was recognised in the Friday *khutba* and coins were minted in her name. When Baghdad was captured, she retreated to southern Iraq.

Turkan Khatun (487/1094): She was a descendant of Afrasyab, and had 10,000 horsemen in her service. She conducted the affairs of state after the death of Malikshah and led the troops in battle. She was called "the master of Isfahan".

Safiyya Khatun (581-640/1167-1242): She was the daughter of the Ayyubid ruler of Aleppo, al-Malik al-'Adil, and administered the authority of state in the name of her young grandson for six years until her death. She is remembered for restoring justice and compassion to the kingdom, and in particular, for eliminating unjust taxes.

It was not only the Central Asian and Turkish dynasties where this happened. For instance, there was Arwa bint Ahmad (d. 532/1136), who acted as ruler of Yemen under the Fatimids there. She is still remembered fondly. She shifted the focus of the country from arms to agriculture, moving the capital from San'a to Jibla.

In Morocco, Zaynab an-Nafzawiyya, the wife of the ruler of the Almoravids, whose dominion extended from North Africa to Spain, is described as *"al-qâ'ima bi mulkihi,"* the one in charge of her husband's domain. Certainly it is clear from the sources that she exercised full authority in all matters of state.

On his travels in the fourteenth century, Ibn Battuta reports his visit to the Maldive Islands where he found a woman, Khadija bint 'Umar al-Bengali, ruling:

> "One of the strange things about these islands is that their ruler is a woman, Khadija. Sovereignty belonged to her grandfather, then to her father and after his death her brother, who was a minor. When he was deposed and put to death some years later, none of the royal house remained but Khadjia and her two younger sisters, so they raised Khadija to the throne."

In the Malay Archipelago in the seventeenth century there were a number of women who succeeded to the thrones of Patani and Acheh, and other sultanates.

✶✳✶✳✶

Carl Petry points out that historians of the Ayyubid and Mamluk periods (566-922/1171-1517) are discovering a remarkable degree of parity between the men and women of the ruling elite. How far down this extended into wider society is unclear. In the cases of *waqfs*, women were quite often chosen to assume exclusive responsibility for property management, i.e. they were trustees and managers of quite substantial properties which served public functions. There are various factors involved in this, but it provides us with some interesting examples.

Amina bint Isma'il: also known as Bint al-Khazin (daughter of the treasurer). After her father's death, the Shafi'i chief qadi had asserted his right to assume control of his trusts of which she was in charge, but the sultan decided in Amina's favour, stating, "I will act for them according to legal principles and shield them against usurpers." Amina managed the properties and trusts she received from her father so prudently that she left "vast assets" at her death.

Mughul: This princess was another respected woman. She was the daughter of the famous qadi and confidential secretary, Nasir ad-din Ibn al-Barizi, and wife of Sultan Jaqmaq. She had previously been married to another qadi. When Jaqmaq died, Mughul took up residence in the home of her daughter's husband, Atabak (supreme commander) Azbak. Azbak so venerated his mother-in-law that when his wife died, he made Mughul guardian of his son, mistress of his house, and manager of his affairs, "even his slave girls". He appointed her *nazira* (overseer) over the *waqfs* of her father, brother and former husband. The historian as-Sayrafi praised her generosity, the *madrasa* that she founded and her support of the poor in Jerusalem. Her funeral was attended by the sultan and most of the royal court. Sultan Qaitbay personally led her funeral prayer and she was buried in the courtyard of the tomb of ash-Shafi'i.

Fatima bint 'Ala' ad-din 'Ali: She was the wife of Sultan Qaitbay. Documents show that she was the supervisor of her brother and sister, and was appointed her father's executor even though there was a surviving son. When she died, she had amassed one of the largest Mamluk fortunes of the ninth/fifteenth century within the *waqfs* that she managed.

Of roughly 1000 *waqf* deeds for the period in the Cairo archives, which were examined by Muhammad Amin, 283 are under a woman's name. One deed is for Tatarkhan, daughter of the Silandar (royal arms bearer), Tashtamur al-Husamai (Rajab 797/1395). The property she managed was large: several hundred faddans (1 faddan = 4,200.8 m^2) of land in the Delta, six town houses, many ships and other rental properties in Cairo.

She is designated as sole supervisor of the estate and guardian of the family's interests. This was fairly typical.

The case of Turkey is also quite interesting. Ibn Battuta visited Bursa while Sultan Orhan was away, and was received by his wife, Nilüfer Khan. Orhan was the son of Osman from whom the Ottomans take their name. Ibn Battuta noted that among the Turks, "The women hold a more dignified position than the men."

Certainly even at the height of the harem system (which was adopted from the Byzantine gynaeceum), we have the 150 year period called the "Reign of Women" from Roxelana, the wife of Suleïman the Magnificent, to the death of Turhan, the mother of Mehmed IV. This was not simply intrigue. They also played a part in affairs of state. Some of the Valide Sultans (Sultan's mothers) corresponded with foreign rulers. There was an interchange between Queen Elizabeth and Valide Safiya, mother of Mehmed III (1595-1693), who is reported as being given "almost full power as regent" for the whole of the Ottoman empire while her son was away on campaigns. In a letter she assures Elizabeth that she was using her influence with her son in connection with the capitulations which had been negotiated. Kosem Mahpeyker acted as regent for the empire in the name of her two sons, Murad IV (1623-1640) and Ibrahim (1640-1648). When Ibrahim was deposed, her power was such that she continued as regent for her grandson Mehmed IV, under the title Buyuk Valide (Grandmother).

Clearly in the past we have instances of women occupying positions in public administration and managing quite well. There were pragmatic reasons for the women's role in such matters among the Mamluks – one of which was the fact that they had a longer life expectancy, given the inherent violence involved in the quest for promotion among the Mamluks. However, when such arrangements were challenged legally, they were upheld as valid. You must note that control of the *waqfs* we have mentioned amounted to control and management of schools, colleges, hospitals, etc. Women also acted as regents in their husband's absence, or in the case of the minority of the heir to the throne. Being the recognised sovereign was more unusual but not unknown.

An interesting point here is that while the West has always criticised Muslim oppression of women, in historical fact the Muslims have produced more female rulers than any other group of people. Even in recent history there have been three Muslim countries with women in leadership positions – Pakistan, Bangladesh and Turkey.

❋❋❋❋❋

Others have looked into the role of women in the modern political arena, based on *Shari'a*. First there is a statement made by the Ikhwan al-Muslimin:

"We now deal with the issue of the woman's right to vote and be elected as a member to representative councils, or to assume public office or carry out professional work. Firstly, women and the right of electing members of representative councils and similar bodies:

"We are of the view that there is nothing in *Shari'a* to prevent women from taking part in these matters. Allah says: *'The men believers and the women believers are responsible for each other. They enjoin the good and forbid the evil.'* (*Surat at-Tawba,* 9:7), and His saying: *'Let there arise out of you a group of people inviting to all that is good and forbidding all evil. And it is they who are the successful.'* (*Surat Al-Imran,* 3:104). This verse includes a command that gives women the right to enjoin the good and forbid the evil and part of this is the right to vote for the representative council in the elections ...

"Secondly, women's membership in representative councils and similar bodies: We are of the view that there is nothing in the *Shari'a* texts to prevent this either. The views we cited earlier concerning their right to vote apply to their right to be elected as well ...

"Thirdly, women's holding of public office: The only public office which it is agreed upon that a woman cannot occupy is the presidency or head of state. As for judiciary office, the jurisprudents have differed over women's holding it. Some, like At-Tabari and Ibn Hazm, said this is permissible without any restrictions. The majority of jurisprudents, however, have forbidden it completely. But there have been those who allowed it for certain types of legal matters and forbade it in others (like the Imam Abu Hanifa). As long as the matter is the subject of interpretation and consideration, it is possible to choose from these opinions in accordance with the fundamentals of the Shari'a, and to achieve the interests of Muslims at large as governed by the Shari'a controls, and also in accordance to the conditions and circumstances of society. As for other types of public office, the woman can accept them as there is nothing in the Shari'a to prevent her from doing so."

So the Ikhwan give wide scope for women's political role – except for the office of head of state. As the position of the Ikhwan has remained theoretical, since they have not come to power, we will end with something more down to earth, part of an interview by Hasan at-Turabi of Sudan, which describes women's political role:

"One of the earliest aims of the movement of Islamic renaissance in this country was to liberate women, although not in terms of western women's liberation, as that could have been a 'fitnah'. However, it could have been a temptation for some if the process of liberation

39

had been delayed for much longer. Eventually this could have led to a breaking away from religion, custom and tradition.

"Although we were small in number, we campaigned very vocally for women's political rights in the Sudan ... Eventually we won the fight, and later on women started coming out into public life. If they had walked the streets dressed like women from other Arab countries, then there would have been a religious and social protest and prohibition against this type of exhibitionism, but women were wearing clothes that were better than the traditional Sudanese dress itself. Some people then tried to claim that the voice of a woman is 'aura', something that should not be heard; however when she started to speak about the Qur'an and Rasul (SAW), men realised it was not their duty to concentrate on her looks, but to ensure her sayings were in accordance with Islam. Eventually men overcame all these complexes and jealousies against the exposure of their wives, daughters or sisters."

In conclusion, we can say that what has come to be the perceived position of women – particularly in the media – has nothing whatsoever to do with either the *deen* itself or with any historical reality. How and why this change has come about in the last three hundred years remains a topic requiring thorough research and precise investigation, and all sorts of factors must be considered in reaching any conclusions about the actual reasons for this change. Nonetheless the truth is that it does not tally with the role of women among the *Salaf*. Of course, women assuming prominent political roles was not universal by any means. It was unusual for a woman to be head of state, but simply that: unusual, not shocking.

As for other public areas of administration – hospitals, schools, trusts, business, and so forth – active women were not unusual at all, and there is nothing in the *deen* to prevent them from being active in these fields. Indeed, it is desirable, because we are all involved in one goal: to establish the *deen* as Allah has commanded in *Surat at-Tawba* (9:71-72):

> *The men and women of the believers are friends of one another. They command the right and forbid the wrong, and establish the prayer and pay* zakat, *and obey Allah and His Messenger. They are the people Allah will have mercy on. Allah is Almighty, All-Wise.*
>
> *Allah has promised the men and women of the believers, Gardens with rivers flowing under them, remaining in them timelessly, for ever, and fine dwellings in the Gardens of Eden. And Allah's good pleasure is greater still. That is the great victory.*

The Spiritual Woman

This heading is somewhat of a misnomer – because as spiritual entities, men and women are the same, and so perhaps this section should be called the 'Spiritual Human Being'. On a spiritual level, there is absolutely no difference between men and women. Allah says in the Qur'an:

> *"Anyone who acts rightly, male or female, being a believer, We will give them a good life and We will recompense them according to the best of what they did."*
> (16:97)

> *"The men and women of the believers are friends of one another. They command the right and forbid the wrong, and establish the prayer and pay* zakat, *and obey Allah and His Messenger. They are the people Allah will have mercy on. Allah is Almighty, All-Wise."* (9:71)

> *"On the Day when you see the believing men and women, with their light streaming out in front of them and to their right: 'Good news for you today of Gardens with rivers flowing under them, remaining in them timelessly forever. That is the Great Victory.'"*
> (57:12)

It is reported in the *Tabaqat* of Ibn Sa'd that the Prophet's wife, Umm Salama, remarked to the Prophet, "Messenger of Allah, women are not mentioned." Whereupon Allah revealed the following *ayat*:

*"Muslim men and Muslim women, believing men and
believing women, obedient men and obedient women,
truthful men and truthful women, steadfast men and
steadfast women, humble men and humble women,
men who give sadaqa and women who give sadaqa,
men who fast and women who fast, men and women
who guard their private parts; men and women who
remember Allah a lot, Allah has prepared forgiveness
for them and an enormous wage."* (33:35)

✳✳✳✳✳

If we are to truly understand the knowledge we study, and if
we are to undertake action which is both beneficial and effective, then we must begin with the spiritual dimension, because
the spiritual underpins all other activity and gives it meaning.
Without awareness of our Creator and a grasp of the illusory
nature of this world, both the individual and society will be dys-
functional – because people will attribute reality to what is
unreal, permanence to what is ephemeral, and authority to that
which in truth has no real authority. Then the human being will
fail to grasp his or her proper role in existence.

So we now need to explore *tasawwuf* – which is the Islamic
term used for the science of dealing with the spiritual dimension in Islam. We cannot do without the spiritual dimension –
which is so frequently neglected in our times – because Allah's
command is for man to WORSHIP Allah and REMEMBER Allah,
first and foremost, and the *Shari'a* is a consequence of this initial command: the *Shari'a* demonstrates how to worship, how
to establish a balanced social nexus and environment, understand the Message, and implement the Message. Thus all our
actions stem from this initial command to worship and remember. Allah says:

> *"I did not create jinn or man except to worship Me."*
> (51:56)

and:

> *"Say: 'Allah misguides anyone He wills and guides to Himself all who turn to Him: those who believe and whose hearts are stilled by remembrance of Allah. Only by remembrance of Allah are hearts made still.'"* (13:27-28)

Allah further cautions those who neglect remembrance of Him:

> *"If someone shuts his eyes to the remembrance of the All Merciful, We assign him a shaytan who becomes his bosom friend. They debar them from the path and yet they still think they are guided."* (43:36-37)

Thus both worship and *dhikr* or remembrance are direct commands of Allah. Worship consists both of outward, physical forms of worship – commands like the prayer, fasting, and *hajj*, and prohibitions like theft, murder, and adultery; and inward actions which are the actions of the heart. There are also commands and prohibitions concerning these activities, and they can be further divided into two categories on the basis of the famous *hadith* found in the *Sahih* collection of Muslim:

> "One day while we were sitting with the Messenger of Allah, may Allah bless him and grant him peace, there appeared before us a man whose clothes were exceedingly white and whose hair was exceedingly black. No signs of journeying were to be seen on him and none of us knew him. He walked up and sat down by the Prophet. Resting his knees against his and placing the palms of his hands on his thighs, he said, 'O Muhammad, tell me about Islam.' The Messenger of

Allah, may Allah bless him and grant him peace, said, 'Islam is to testify that there is no god but Allah and Muhammad is the Messenger of Allah, to perform the prayers, to pay the *zakat*, to fast in Ramadan, and to make the pilgrimage to the House if you are able to do so.' He said, 'You have spoken the truth.' We were astonished at him asking him and saying that he had spoken the truth. He said, 'Then tell me about belief.' He said, 'It is to believe in Allah, His angels, His Books, His Messengers, and the Last Day, and to believe in the Decree, both the good and evil of it.' He said, 'You have spoken the truth.' He said, 'Then tell me about *ihsan*.' He said, 'It is to worship Allah as though you are seeing Him. Even if you do not see Him, He sees you.'"

In the end the Prophet informed them that it was Jibril (Gabriel) who had come to teach them their religion *(deen)*.

So there is *iman*, belief in Allah and His angels, Books, Messengers, the Last Day and the Decree, which provides an accurate and truthful blueprint for a view of a multi-dimensional universe which includes both the spiritual and physical worlds.

Then there is *ihsan*, which consists of honing and purifying the inward which leads to recognition of what the self is, its position in the cosmos and how it can be purified completely. There are commands which demand certain inward qualities like sincerity (*ikhlas*), truthfulness (*sidq*) and trust in Allah (*tawakkul*), and there are prohibitions of blameworthy traits like hypocrisy, pride, envy, rancour, and showing off to impress people. These are all part of the inward discipline which is just as necessary as the outward, physical actions. Allah has commanded us to take care of the inward as well as the outward.

The inward is, in fact, the more important of the two, because the inward provides the foundation for the outward. Actions spring from intentions, which are shaped by awareness and knowledge. This is why the Prophet pointed out the importance of training the heart to his Companions. He said, 'There is a piece of flesh in the body. If it is in order, the entire body is in order. If it is corrupt, then the entire body is corrupt. It is the heart." (al-Bukhari and Muslim). He also said, "Allah does not look at your bodies nor at your forms, but He looks at your hearts." (Muslim). And Allah says: *"The Day when neither wealth nor sons will be of any help, except to those who bring to Allah sound, flawless hearts."* (26:88-89). Thus the importance of the heart is paramount.

In fact, this concern and attention to the state of the heart is an individual obligation (*fard 'ayn*). It is something which each and every one of us is required to undertake. Allah says: *"My Lord has forbidden indecency, both open and secret."* (7:33). Commentators explain that inward indecencies are things like envy, rancour, hypocrisy, and so forth. There are many *hadiths* to this effect.

How then can one discipline the heart and purify it of all these disastrous feelings which it experiences? The Islamic technique for this purification is known as *tasawwuf*.

Now at this point, some people are going to have a reflex reaction and automatically attack Sufism or *tasawwuf*. This is because in recent times *tasawwuf* has found itself under attack by those who call themselves 'traditionalists' or 'Salafis' (which is in itself a modern term borrowed from the past by Muhammad 'Abduh), but who are in fact modernists. Therefore it is first necessary to establish the position and validity of Sufism within Islam. The actual *Salaf*, the first three generations of the Muslim *Umma*, would be astonished at the necessity of doing this, but nonetheless it seems that we need to re-establish the fact that Sufism is an integral part of Islam and always has been.

In the course of this discussion, Ibn Taymiyya in particular is cited. This is because the Salafis and Wahhabis have misused him in their condemnation of Sufism, for he was also a Sufi and a member of the Qadiriyya *tariqa*.

✳✳✳✳✳

Historically, the starting point of Sufism is found in Islamic *zuhd* (asceticism or making do without what is unnecessary), and scrupulousness (*war'*), which in the course of time eventually developed into what we call Sufism. It is often said that in the early days, Sufism was a reality without a name and in recent times it often becomes a name without a reality. The predilection for *zuhd* was based on the command of the Prophet. For instance Sahl ibn Sa'id reported:

> "A man came to the Messenger of Allah, may Allah bless him and grant him peace, and said, 'Messenger of Allah, show me an action which will make Allah love me and people love me if I do it.' He said, 'Do without in this world and Allah will love you. Do without in what people have, and people will love you!'" (Ibn Majah)

He also said:

> "This world is accursed and what it contains is accursed – except for remembrance of Allah and what pleases Him, a scholar or a learner." (at-Tirmidhi and Ibn Majah)

There are numerous *hadiths* and *ayats* of the Qur'an which stress the importance of not becoming attached to this world. Volumes of them could be cited. This is, in fact, what Sufism is: pursuing this path which the Prophet, may Allah bless him and grant him peace, indicated should be pursued. Ibn Taymiyya defines *tasawwuf* in his *Majmu'a Fatawa* as follows:

47

"The use of the word *tasawwuf* has been thoroughly discussed. Among those who spoke about *tasawwuf* are not just the Imams and Shaykhs, but also they include Ahmad ibn Hanbal, Abu Sulayman ad-Darani, as-Saqati, al-Junayd al-Baghdadi, al-Hasan al-Basri, Ma'ruf al-Karkhi, 'Abdu'l-Qadir al-Jilani, al-Bistami and many others. This is a term that was given to those who were dealing with that kind of science.

"Some people have criticised *Sufiyya* and *tasawwuf* and have said that they are innovators, outside the *Sunna*, but the truth is they are striving in Allah's obedience, just as others of Allah's People have striven in Allah's obedience. So from among them you will find the Foremost in Nearness by virtue of his striving. And some of them are from the People of the Right hand [*Sura Waqi'a*], but slower in their progress. As regards both kinds, they might exercise *ijtihad,* and in that case they might be correct or they might be wrong. And from both groups, some of them might commit a sin and repent. And this is the origin of *tasawwuf*. And from that origin, it has been spread."

If you want to throw out Sufism and anything remotely 'Sufi', then in effect, you must discard all of the four schools and at least 75% of the major corpus of knowledge that has come down to us from prior generations of scholars – because the people who transmitted this to us were mainly Sufis or taught by Sufis. Such a rejection is the logical outcome of the course that many modernists are following, who, for example, assert that in this modern age it is not necessary to follow a *madhhab*, thereby creating a fifth *madhhab*, which did not exist in the time of the original *Salaf*.

A brief mention of some of the outstanding scholars of Islam will illustrate the fact that Sufism is deeply embedded in the fabric of Islam:

Imam Abu Hanifa (d. 150/767)

Ibn 'Abidin relates in *ad-Durr al-Mukhtar* that Imam Abu Hanifa stated: "If it were not for two years, I would have perished." Ibn 'Abidin comments: For two years he accompanied Ja'far as-Sadiq and he acquired the spiritual knowledge that made him a gnostic in the Way ... Abu 'Ali Daqqaq received the path from Abu al-Qasim al-Nasirabadi, who received it from ash-Shibli, who received it from Sari al-Saqati who received it from al-Ma'ruf al-Karkhi, who received it from Dawud at-Ta'i, who received the knowledge, both the external and the internal, from Imam Abu Hanifa.

Imam Malik (d. 179/95)

Imam Malik explicitly enjoined *tasawwuf* as a duty of scholars in his statement: "He who practices *tasawwuf* without learning *fiqh* corrupts his faith, while he who learns *fiqh* without practising *tasawwuf* corrupts himself. Only he who combines the two proves true." ['Ali al-Adawi, vol. 2, p 195.]

Imam ash-Shafi'i (d. 204//820)

Imam ash-Shafi'i said: "Three things in this world have been made dear to me: avoiding affectation, treating people kindly, and following the Path of the people of *tasawwuf*." [al-'Ajluni, *Kashf al-khafa*, 1:341]

Imam Ahmad ibn Hanbal (d. 241/855)

He said to his son 'Abdullah, "O my son, you must sit with the people of *tasawwuf*, because they will provide you with increased knowledge, watchfulness, fear of

Allah, asceticism and lofty resolve." [*Tanwir al-Qulub,* p. 405]

Muhammad ibn Ahmad as-Saffarini al-Hanbali (d. 1188) relates in *Ghidha' al-Albab* that Imam Ahmad said about the Sufis: "I do not know people better than them." Someone said to him: "But they listen to music and they reach states of ecstasy." He said: "Let them enjoy an hour with Allah." [as-Saffarini, *Ghidha' al-Albab,* 1:120]

Some other major scholars associated with Sufism are:

Jalal ad-Din as-Suyuti (d. 911/1505)

As-Suyuti, said in his book on *tasawwuf* entitled *Ta'yid al-Haqiqa*: "*Tasawwuf* in itself is a most honourable knowledge. It explains how to follow the *Sunna* of the Prophet and to leave innovation, how to purify the self ... and submit to Allah truly ...

"I have looked at the matters concerning which the Imams of *Shari'a* have criticised the Sufis, and I did not see a single true Sufi holding such positions. Rather, they are held by the people of innovation and the extremists who have claimed for themselves the title of Sufi – while in reality they are not ..."

Imam an-Nawawi (d. 676/ 1277)

Imam an-Nawawi is one of the great scholars, *hadith* masters, and meticulously accurate jurists of the Shafi'i school. His books are considered to be authoritative in the methodology of the law, Qur'an commentary, and *hadith*. An-Nawawi himself was a Sufi who has various books on *tasawwuf.*

Ibn Taymiyya (d. 728/ 1328)

Ibn Taymiyya's Sufi inclinations and his reverence for Shaykh 'Abdu'l-Qadir al-Jilani can be seen in his hundred page commentary on *Futuh al-Ghayb* – and the fact that he actually wrote a commentary on this Sufic text demonstrates that he considered *tasawwuf* to be essential within the life of the Islamic community.

Ibn Taymiyya is also notorious for his condemnation of Ibn al-'Arabi. However, what he condemned was not Ibn al-'Arabi himself, but one of his books, *Fusus al-Hikam,* whose nuances he did not understand. As for Ibn al-'Arabi's major work, *al-Futuhat al-Makkiyya,* Ibn Taymiyya had great appreciation for it as he declared in a letter to al-Munayji (d. 709/1309).

We could go on and on: Ibn 'Abdin, Ibn Hajar al-Haytami, 'Abdu'l-Ghani an-Nabulisi, as-Subki, al-Hakim at-Tirmidhi, at-Tabarani, al-Ghazali, al-Bayhaqi, al-Baydawi, Ibn Khaldun, Ibn Qayyim al-Jawziyya, ash-Shatibi, and so on.

This is not, of course, to condone some of the more extreme practices and manifestations which have sprung up by some who call themselves 'Sufis'. We are talking about Sufism clearly set in the context of the Book and the *Sunna.* The blanket condemnation of the Sufis by some of the modernists really amounts to the claim that the *deen* has not been properly understood by anyone since the Prophet and the early community – and themselves. In effect, they are implying that everyone before them was wrong. As al-Hasan al-Basri (d. 110/728) said, "Two innovations have appeared in Islam: a man of bad judgement who holds that the Garden will be the reward only for those who see eye to eye with him; and a man of luxury and extravagance who worships this world ... Reject these two for they are doomed to the Fire."

Such an attitude is contrary to the instructions of the Prophet, may Allah bless him and grant him peace, who commanded us to follow the Community, the *Jama'a*. He said, "Hold to the consensus of the Muslims." What consensus is better than those of these past scholars? That indeed is the Sufi position. Ash-Shatibi (d. 790/1388), the famous Maliki *faqih* who dealt with *usul al-fiqh*, said:

> "Their chief spokesman and the master of their ways and pillar of their group, Abu'l-Qasim al-Qushayri, declared that they acquired the name of *tasawwuf* in order to dissociate themselves from the people of innovation. He mentioned that the most honourable of Muslims after the Prophet did not give themselves, in their time, any other title than Companions, as there is no merit above that of being a Companion – then those who followed them were called the Followers. After that the people varied and the disparity of levels among them became more apparent. The elite, among whom prudence in belief was intense, were then called *zuhhad* and 'worshippers'. Subsequently all kinds of innovations made their appearance, and the elite of the *Ahl as-Sunna* who observed their obligations with Allah and preserved their hearts from heedlessness became unique in their kind under the name of *tasawwuf*." [ash-Shatibi, *al-I'tisam*]

So what is Sufism? Why did these scholars of Islam consider it so essential? As Ibn Taymiyya said, it involves the purification of the self and the quest for achieving what the Prophet described as *'ihsan'* which is part of *ikhlas*, sincerity in worshipping Allah. Sincerity lies at the very heart of the *deen*. *Ikhlas* means making your actions purely for the sake of Allah and not for any reward or for the good opinion of someone else. We are commanded to make our *deen* sincerely for Allah frequently in the Qur'an: *"So call upon Allah, making the* deen *sincerely His, even though the unbelievers detest it."* (40:14)

Ibn 'Ata'llah says in the *Hikam*:

"Actions are merely propped-up shapes.
Their life-breath is the presence
of the secret of sincerity in them."

Commenting on this Ibn 'Ajiba says: "All actions are shapes and forms. Their life-breath is the existence of sincerity in them. As mere forms cannot stand without a life-breath, for they will be dead and inert, so too the actions of the body and the heart only stand because of something within them. Otherwise they are merely propped-up shapes and empty forms of no worth." [*Iqaz al-Himam*, 1:25]

Thus the heart must be in tune with actions – and this requires purification. The science of how to purify the heart, so that it is constantly aware of the presence of God, is *tasawwuf*. The desire to reject the basis of this science is a desire to separate the spirit of Islam from its body, and to ignore the third of the three pillars mentioned in the *hadith* of Jibril, *ihsan*. Thus it is, in fact, a desire to abandon Islam as practised by the *Salaf*, in exchange for a 'modern' re-defined version which is acceptable to those who reject Allah and His Messenger, may Allah bless him and grant him peace.

If an objection is made about the terms used by the Sufis, like *shari'a*, *tariqa*, and *haqiqa*, or *fana'* and *baqa'*, they are simply technical terms developed by those skilled in this science, just as the scholars of *hadith* or any other science have developed a whole technical language which they use to describe and explain their science. I have not heard anyone saying that we have to discard terms like *sahih*, *hasan*, *gharib*, *asbab an-nuzul*, etc., because they were not used in the time of the Prophet, may Allah bless him and grant him peace. That would be completely ludicrous.

Criticism is also made of certain methods of *dhikr*, "because they were not done in the time of the Prophet or the

Companions." They are techniques which have developed in respond to the needs of the people. Guns did not exist in the time of the Prophet nor did aeroplanes, cars, trains, electricity, laser surgery, or television.

This is not the place for a detailed exposition of the science of *tasawwuf* itself, but I will make a few further comments on what it is to avoid any misapprehensions. To quote Ahmad az-Zarruq, the great Maliki scholar, *faqih* and Sufi:

> "Aspects of Sufism which are defined, delineated and explained amount to about two thousand. All of them amount to sincerity in turning to Allah Almighty, of which they are facets, and Allah knows best." He goes on, "There is no *tasawwuf* except through understanding *fiqh,* since the outward judgements of Allah are only known through it. There is no *fiqh* without *tasawwuf* since actions are only according to sincerity." [*Qawa'id at-Tasawwuf*, p. 2]

Ash-Shar'ani said:

> "The path of the Sufis is based on the Book and *Sunna*, and based on the behaviour of the Prophets and the righteous. It is not blamed unless it differs from something which is clear in the Qur'an, *Sunna* or consensus. If it does not differ, then the most that can be said about it is that it is an understanding given to a Muslim man. Whoever wishes may act on it and whoever wishes may leave it ... There is no way to condemn it except by the bad opinion of people, or accusing them of showing off." [*at-Tasawwuf al-Islami*]

Hajji Khalifa says in *Kashf adh-Dhunun*:

"The science of *tasawwuf* can also be called the science of the Reality. It is the science of the Path (*Tariqa*) which is the purification of the self from base qualities and the purification of the heart from base desires. The science of Shari'a without the Reality is void and the science of the Reality without the Shari'a is void."

Ash-Sha'rani said: "The science of *tasawwuf* designates a knowledge which ignites in the hearts of the *awliya'* when they illuminate the Book and *Sunna* by action."

Sahl at-Tustari said: "Our fundamentals are seven: holding to the Book of Allah Almighty, following the *Sunna* of His Messenger, eating the *halal*, refraining from causing harm, avoiding sins, repentance, and fulfilling the rights of others."

Another aspect of Sufism which we must mention is its strong connection with *jihad* and *da'wa*. Historically it is the Sufis who have frequently carried out the *jihad* against the unbelievers. The extent of the activity of the Sufis in *jihad* is not surprising since the goal of *tasawwuf* is sincerity in one's devotion to Allah, and sincerity leads to wholehearted devotion to the Cause of Allah. They were instrumental in spreading and defending the *deen* because the aim is to actualise *ihsan* as described by the Prophet, may Allah bless him and grant him peace: "It is to worship Allah as though you are seeing Him. Even if you do not see Him, He sees you." They realise the truth of the words of Allah Almighty:

> *"Say: 'If your fathers or your sons or your brothers or your wives or your tribe, or any wealth you have acquired, or any business you fear may slump, or any dwelling-places which please you, are dearer to you than Allah and His Messenger and doing jihad in His way, then wait until Allah brings about His command. Allah does not guide degenerate people.'"* (9:24)

55

and so nothing is dearer to them than Allah and His Messenger and doing *jihad* in His Way.

Look briefly at the great *jihads* against the unbelievers and colonialists of recent history: on the whole, they have been undertaken by Sufis, not by those modernists who, supported by the colonialists and bankers, generally fight against other Muslims. Here are a few examples, although this list is by no means inclusive:

- **Bosnia:** In Bosnia, a great revival of Sufism has occurred both prior to and during the recent war. In the late 70's through the 80's Sufism enjoyed a small revival, which has grown now as a result of the war. Many shaykhs of the Naqshbandiyya and Qadiriyya have been active in Eastern Europe in reviving the spirit of Islam and *jihad* during this time.

- **Daghestan:** the Naqshbandi Shaykh Shamil fought the Tsarist Russians for 35 years in the Caucasus. He was never defeated.

- **Chechnya:** Sufism is central to the Chechens, and indeed throughout the North Caucasus, the Turkmen steppes, and the Ferghana valley in Central Asia. In short, wherever the Russians have met massive popular resistance, it has been Sufi *tariqas* who organised and led the fight. In the 1960's the Russians discovered that the Sufi *tariqas* which they had tried to suppress had not disappeared – they had gone underground and were re-emerging. It was also the Qadiriyya who converted the Ingush in the 1870's, an area which had not been touched by Islam until then. One source says, "Between 1877 and the 1917 revolution, almost all of the adult population of Chechnia-Ingushetia belonged either to the Naqshbaniyya or to the Qadiriyya *tariqa*." The same was more or less true of Daghestan.

- **Nigeria**: There was the famous *jihad* of 'Uthman dan Fodio against the pagans in Nigeria from 1804 to 1808 and the founding of the Sokoto khalifate. He was a shaykh of the Qadiriyya *tariqa* and has numerous books on Sufism.

- **Algeria:** There was the famous *jihad* of 'Abdu'l-Qadir al-Jaza'iri of the Qadiriyya *tariqa* against the French from 1832 to 1847.

- **China:** Ma Hualong led the Naqshbandi order and other Hui Muslims into open revolt against the Chinese between 1862 and 1876. Hualong was executed by the Chinese in 1871. Sufism became more secretive and dispersed after this confrontation. Today over 125,000 Hui still follow the Naqshbandi *tariqa* in north-western China. It would be interesting to find out the level of Sufi involvement in the current Uighur unrest in Xinjiang.

- **Libya:** The Sanusi *tariqa*, of which Umar al-Mukhtar was a member, led the fight against the Italians. They were banned in 1980 by Gadhafi, but are still playing a large part in the opposition against him. Also the efforts of the founder of the Sanusiyya, Muhammad 'Ali as-Sanusi, from 1807 to 1859 consolidated Islam as the religion of the Libyan desert.

- **Mauritania:** Ma' al-'Aynayn al-Qalqami, a Qadiriyya Sufi shaykh, fought against the incursions of the French in northern Mauritania and southern Morocco from 1905 to 1909. There were other Mauritanian Sufis involved in the fight as well.

- **Senegal:** al-Hajj 'Umar Tal, a Tijani shaykh led the *jihad* against the French and pagans in Guinea, Senegal and Mali from 1852 to 1864.

- **Somalia:** Muhammad 'Abdullah as-Somali, a shaykh of the Sahiliyya *tariqa* led the resistance against the British and Italians in his country from 1899 to 1920. It was one of the longest sustained and successful resistance movements in

Africa in the 19th and early 20th century, thanks largely to the cohesion provided by the *tariqa*.

- **Sudan:** The movement of Muhammad Ahmad ibn 'Abdullah al-Mahdi against the British in the late 19th century is famous.

- **Egypt:** The Darqawi al-Hajj Muhammad al-Ahrash fought the French in Egypt in 1799.

Sufism also played a large part in the spread of Islam in the Indian sub-continent, Indonesia, Malaysia, and sub-Saharan Africa. At the turn of the century, the Qadiri Shaykh Uways al-Barawi helped to spread Islam west and inland from the East African coast. Under the Ottomans, the Naqshbandiyya and Qadiriya established the *deen* in the Balkans. Sufis also played a part in the spread of Islam in the Malay archipelago.

✽✽✽✽✽

Now, as this is ostensibly about 'the Spiritual Woman,' it should be pointed out that Sufism is not confined to men, but open to women as well. The first major female figure in *tasawwuf* was Rabi'a al-Adawiyya (95-185/713-801). Rabi'a's starting point was neither a fear of hell nor a desire for paradise, but only love. "God is God," she said, "for this I love God ... not because of any gifts, but for Himself." We also have some wonderful stories about her and her contemporary, al-Hasan al-Basri. Al-Hasan al-Basri said about her: "I passed one whole night and day with Rabi'a, speaking of the Way and the Truth, and it never passed through my mind that I was a man nor did it occur to her that she was a woman, and at the end when I looked at her I saw myself as spiritually bankrupt and Rabi'a as truly sincere."

There is also the famous tale where Hasan comes and casts his carpet on the water and sits on the water, calling on Rabi'a to come and converse with him. She throws hers into the air, flies up to it and sitting there, says, "O Hasan, come up here where people can see us better." Hasan is silent and then Rabi'a says, "Hasan, what you did a fish can do ... and what I did a fly can do. The real work is beyond both of these."

On another occasion she asked another Sufi, Rabah al-Qaysi, "Are the nights and days long for you?" "Why should they be?" he asked. She said, "Because of your yearning to behold Allah." When he heard this, he was silent and Rabi'a said, "The answer is 'Yes' for me."

One spring day Rabi'a was in her room and her servant called, "Come out and see what the Creator has made!" Rabi'a replied, "Rather come in and see the Creator! The contemplation of the Creator preoccupies me and so I do not care to contemplate what He has created."

Throughout the centuries, women have continued to be active in *tasawwuf*, often less visible and less outspoken than men, but no less active. Many of the famous shaykhs had female teachers, students, and friends who greatly influenced them.

Ibn al-'Arabi (560-638/1165-1240), tells about the time he spent with two elderly women Sufis who had a profound influence on him: Shams of Marchena and Fatima of Cordoba.

Someone for whom al-Bistami (d. 260/874) had great regard was Fatima of Nishapur (d. 223/838), of whom he said, "There was no station (on the Way) about which I told her that she had not already passed beyond." Someone once asked the great Egyptian Sufi master Dhu'n-Nun al-Misri, "Who do you think is the highest among the Sufis?" He replied, "A woman in Makka, called Fatima of Nishapur, whose discourse displays a profound grasp of the inner meanings of the Qur'an." He said about her, "She is one of the saints of Allah, and my teacher." Abu Hafs al-Haddad (d. 264/878) who had learned from other women before he met her, said, "I saw that the Almighty grants knowledge and gnosis to whomever He pleases."

The *Tabaqat al-Kubra* of ash-Sha'rani has a section devoted to women which mentions some of the women Sufis of whom he was aware. In it he mentions: Mu'adha al-'Adawiya, who transmitted from 'A'isha, performed 600 *rak'ats* a day, and, after the death of her husband, never went to bed to sleep; Rabi'a al-'Adawiya whom we have already mentioned; Majida al-Qurashiyya, who tried to be constantly aware of death so that she would not fall into heedlessness; 'A'isha bint Ja'far as-Sadiq, who was dominated by hope for Allah's grace; the wife of Rabah al-Qaysi, who used to pray the entire night and then wake up her husband at dawn to pray; Fatima an-Nisaburi, whom we have already mentioned; Rabi'a bint Isma'il, who said, "I do not hear the *adhan* without remembering the Summons of the Day of Resurrection. I do not see snow without remembering the pages of the books (of people's actions). I do not feel heat but that I remember the Final Gathering."

He also mentions Umm Harun, who ate only bread and prayed all night long; 'Amra, the wife of Habib (another Sufi), who prayed all the night and would wake up her husband before dawn, saying, "Wake up, man. Night has gone and day has come. The star of the Highest Assembly has dispersed and the caravans of the righteous have departed and you are too late to catch them."

There was also Amatu'l-Jalil, to whom the Sufis of the time went to resolve a dispute over the definition of *wilaya*. She told them, "If anyone tells you that the *wali* of Allah has any preoccupation except Allah Almighty, call him a liar." There was also 'Abida bint Abi Kilab. Once she heard someone say, "The God-fearing does not achieve true fear of Allah until he longs for nothing more than to be presented before Allah," and she fainted. There was also Hafira al-'Abida, to whom the people of her time came to ask for supplication.

There was also the Persian Sha'wana, who constantly wept. Men and women gathered around her to hear her discourses. She said, "The weeper weeps because of what he knows of himself and what he has done and what he is travelling to."

Someone remarked about her, "Since the time my eyes fell upon Sha'wana, I have never inclined to worldly things because of her blessing and I have never undervalued any of the Muslims."

There was also Amina ar-Ramliyya. Bishr ibn al-Harith (d. 226/841), a well-known Sufi, used to visit her. Bishr fell ill and she visited him. While she was there, Ahmad ibn Hanbal came in to visit him and asked Bishr, "Who is this?" He replied, "This is Amina ar-Ramliyya. She heard I was ill and has come to visit me." He asked Bishr to ask her to make supplication for him.

There are many, many examples right across the Muslim world, for instance Fatima or Jahan-Ara, the favourite daughter of Shah Jahan, the Mogul emperor of India (1592-1666). Fatima wrote a book on *tasawwuf* called *Risala-i Sahibiyya*.

'A'isha of Damascus was one of the well-known mystics of the fifteenth century. She wrote a famous commentary on al-Ansari's *Stations on the Way (Manazil as-Sa'irin)* entitled *Veiled Hints*. She also has a *diwan*, or collection of poems. There have been and are many other women Sufis, particularly in Morocco and Mauritania.

To move on to a more modern note which involves women, Sufism and *jihad*, we will turn to Algeria. Among the Ait Isma'il of the Jurjura Mountains in the Kabylia there were several instances of female leadership in the Sufi *zawiyyas*, particularly among the Rahmaniyya *Tariqa*. In their central *zawiyya*, the shaykh died in 1836-37 and his widow, Lalla Khadija took over the leadership. In the next decade, her eldest daughter, Lalla Fatima, the wife of the new Rahmaniyya shaykh, emerged as a leader during the French assault on the Jurjura Mountains between 1856 and 1857. Lalla Fatima not only organised armed resistance against the colonial army but also fought alongside the men. Another instance of Sufism and *jihad* combined.

There is also the case of Lalla Zaynab bint Muhammad, well-documented by Julia Clancy-Smith. She was born in al-

Hamil, Algeria, around 1850. Al-Hamil is the location of the Rahmaniyya *zawiyya* of Sidi Muhammad b. Abi Qasim (1823-97), which was very affluent at that time, as it was tolerated by the French because Sidi Muhammad was not interested in politics. He died in June 1897 and the French assumed that leadership, as a matter of course, would go to his nephew, Muhammad ibn al-Hajj Muhammad, who was well-disposed to the French. They had failed to take account of the shaykh's daughter Lalla Zaynab (c. 1850-1904). She took over the running of the *zawiyya* herself, assuming all the responsibilities for education and social welfare, despite intense opposition from the Bureau Arabe officers in Bou Saada who backed her cousin.

The centre provided refuge to a number of people, political refugees from the 1864 revolt of the Sidi Auad Shaykh (western Algeria) and from the 1871 Muqrani uprising (north-western Algeria). Lalla Zaynab probably gained her knowledge of how the colonial system functioned from these refugees. When she took over the *zawiyya* in 1897, she was very conversant with how it operated. Her father had taken great care with her education. He had centralised the operations and finances and had always kept Zaynab well-informed. In 1877, while she was in her twenties, the shaykh made a will in favour of Zaynab and his other children. Zaynab was singled out as receiving a "portion equal to a male".

When her cousin tried to take over, Zaynab took the keys to the buildings and coffers, and forbade the students and staff of the *zawiyya* to obey his commands. The cousin tried to establish a counter school. After a whole year he had only managed to gather thirty students.

Ironically, it was the local French colonial officials who were the most vehemently opposed to Lalla Zaynab, because she was a woman. Meanwhile she lodged a complaint against them with those at the top of colonial authority in Algeria. At this time, the Governor General was Jules Cambon who was attempting to soften the regime's hostile stance towards the Sufi orders. She effectively checkmated the moves of the local colonial office. This is yet another instance of the close relationship between *tasawwuf* and *jihad*.

We also hear about an Algerian woman presenting a demand to a Bureau Arabe official in 1849. When the officers were slow to respond, she threatened to go to her Shaykh since she was a Sufi.

✻✻✻✻✻

A final word about Sufism. It is not an 'ism' or an 'ology'. It is not an ideology. It is a science. If you prefer a more modern label, you might call it Islamic behavioural psychology. *Tasawwuf* amounts to realising the Shari'a in the arena of action and behaviour and making it part of you until you are transformed by it. If you are it, that's it. The science of *tasawwuf* is the means to this end, the hidden fruit of which is gnosis. It is internalising a vibrant awareness of *tawhid*, the oneness of God, at what might be termed a cellular level. Allah says: *"Allah never changes a people's state unless they change what is in themselves."* (13:11)

This is the transformation of the self which forms the basis for a larger change in society. It is real activism. Hence the connection between inward and outward *jihad*.

On one hand, the self is the worst and basest thing in the world, but on the other, it is the most sublime and tremendous locus for wisdom. In the words of the famous saying attributed to Yahya ibn Ma'ad ar-Razi,"Whoever knows himself knows his Lord." Knowledge of the faults of the self is a means to purification, and purification is a means to recognition and knowledge of the Creator of the self.

The attack against Sufism has come from two fronts. One is from the orientalists who maintain that nothing as profound and fertile as *tasawwuf* could have come from something as 'barren' as Islam. In other words, their attack stems from an arrogant denigration of Islam which is rooted in their 'self'-ish desire to have a reason to justify their rejection of the truth of Islam.

The other attack is from modernism – which while claiming to be 'traditional' is, in fact, a modern ideology nurtured and encouraged among the Muslims by the colonialists and orientalists in order to weaken and undermine them, and which relies on insecurity and ignorance. Because it is based on insecurity and lack of knowledge, it is intolerant and consists of rhetoric, argumentation and condemnation. You cannot build on that – you can only destroy.

As well as the inability to grasp the fact that the course that they are pursuing actually weakens and divides the Muslims rather than strengthening and uniting them, what is really lacking in modernist movements in Islam is the revival of the inward, spiritual life which is the life-breath of Islam. 'Islam' has for many become little more than a carefully erected modern concrete structure adorned with expensive chandeliers and carpets – a prison in disguise, without true brotherhood and without love for fellow Muslims. There is no scope for growth in such a scenario.

Fortunately, there is another scenario which is possible: Living Islam, embodied by living Muslims, both men and women, who bring the knowledge contained in books to life through actions based on clear intentions and wisdom, trusting in Allah and fearing only Allah, establishing not only the five pillars of Islam, but also embodying the vibrancy which comes from spiritual enlightenment.

And it is the people who are sincerely concerned with the purification of their hearts who will, *insha' llah*, transform society, because it is the transformation of the self which forms the basis for a larger change in society. If the self is darkened, society suffers. If the self is illuminated, society flourishes. If the self is darkened society suffers. If the self is illuminated, society flourishes. What is desired is the empowerment of both men and women through recognition that there is no power nor strength except from Allah.

Abu Yazid al-Bistami was asked to describe the Sufi and said:

"He is the one who takes the Book of Allah in his right hand and the *Sunna* in his left hand, looks with one of his eyes at the Garden and the other at the Fire, binds himself with the wrapper of this world and cloaks himself with the cloak of the Next world, and between them says to his Master, 'At Your service, O Allah. At Your service'.

❋❋❋❋❋

"The only one who needs the proof and seeks light by the candle is the one who is in the darkness of night. When the day breaks, and dawn rises and shines, he does not need a lamp or a candle."

Sidi 'Ali al-Jamal

And the last of our prayer is: Praise be to Allah, the Lord of the worlds. There is no great power and no strength but through Allah, the Mighty, the Great. My help is only with Allah. In Him I have put my trust – and to Him I turn in renewal. Praise belongs to Allah for the blessing of Islam, and it is blessing enough.

❋❋❋❋❋